MW01105098

In Darkness and in Light

A Physician's Journey into Spiritual Healing

Lesley B. Heafitz, M.D.

First Person Press

Swampscott, Massachusetts

For information contact:
First Person Press
25 Allen Road
Swampscott, Massachusetts 01907
(617) 593-4362

Editor: Barbara Wolf
Cover design: Leslie Haimes

Cover photograph: Harold Summers
Copyright © Harold Summers

Fourth Printing, 1995
ISBN 0-9635307-3-9
Printed in the United States of America

To my devoted husband and soul mate,
this book is lovingly dedicated.

❧

PREFACE

I realize now that when I chose a career in medicine, I had no clear concept of healing. It was not until I was diagnosed with ovarian cancer, three years ago, that I began to understand. Far more than physical cure, recovery from disease is a process involving mind, body and spirit, in a continuum through darkness into light.

My own path has involved so much more than the goal of permanent remission. In my efforts to heal, I am undergoing a process of personal exploration and growth, a journey that has taught me over and again to live in the moment, to accept who I am and what is now.

Many of the poems in this book were drawn from guided visualizations which formed an integral part of my healing. A form of meditation, guided visualization occurs in an altered mind state, assisted by a healer. Writing became a part of my process, and these poems were written originally just for me. However, as I reread them, they spoke to me, not only as the patient, but as the physician and healer. I feel they have something to offer others who are on a healing journey. Whether your pathway involves disease or a search for self understanding, it is my hope that you may find the inspiration in these pages to lead you, too, from darkness into light.

ACKNOWLEDGMENTS

Someone once said that when you are combating cancer, you must pick one captain for your team – and stick with that person. For me, that captain has been my surgeon, Dr. Arlan Fuller, who has given me life. My coach has been my very dear friend and healer, Marc Clopton, who inspires me to play. Finally, my cheering squad has been my husband and six children, without whose support I could not have played the game so far. To each and every one of these people, I am eternally grateful.

I would also like to thank Rhina P. Espaillat and the other members of the Pow Wow River Poets who have been most encouraging to me as a budding poet and who have helped me edit some of the poems in this book. I would like to extend my gratitude to the National Library of Poetry for publishing my poem, "In Darkness and in Light," in its anthology, *A Break in the Clouds*, and to the Harvard Medical Alumni Bulletin, in which my poems, "Doubts and Cowardice," "Invincible," "No Place to Heal," and "Patient's Plea," appeared as part of a published address I delivered at Harvard Medical School's Alumni Day in June, 1992.

Finally, I am grateful to Barbara Wolf, my good friend, editor, and publisher, who has borne with me patiently and proddingly, and whose efforts have turned the publication of this book from a dream into reality.

IN
DARKNESS
AND IN
LIGHT

IN DARKNESS AND IN LIGHT

Enshadowed and illumined,

In darkness and in light,

I travel on a journey without end.

Doubt imbued in me since earliest childhood

Settles as a darkening cloud

Around my consciousness,

Until a shaft of guiding light penetrates my heart.

Expanding there, it grows,

And slowly clears away the clouds,

To illuminate for me

The soul-sensed vision of an awesome dream.

The fog closes in again.

Engulfed in murky shadows,

I seek and find, once more,

That luminescent beam that beckons me

To follow guardian angels

Ever upward to that place

Whence will come the Power of the Light,

Enabling me to do the work of God.

HEALING THE DISEASE

"IT'S MALIGNANT"

"It's malignant," the surgeon said.
Two words with cutting edge
Go through me.
Like his scalpel,
They assault my fate.
First the anger, then the tears...
Then I vow, I'll win this fight.

YOM KIPPUR PRAYER

In awe

I stand before you, God.

Alone,

Without mother, without father,

Poised between life and death,

I ask only for a second chance.

There's so much for me here:

My beloved husband,

My dearest children, not yet grown.

Please, I beg you,

Grant me more time –

Time for love,

Time for living.

Hear my simple prayer,

And on this Day of Judgement

Let my name be written

In the Book of Life!

DOUBTS AND COWARDICE

Tears soak my pillow,
They hurt my head.
I want so, to go on living,
But I am caught,
I can't decide
How to best remain alive.

If they pour more poison into me,
I fear I may yet cease to be.
I begin to feel so broken now –
More than my hair has fallen out.
Where is my strength, fight and vigor
Which conquered illness and made me heal?
What is this cowardice I feel?
It was not there before,
When I was fighting for my life
And won.

Will this be death when the war is over,
As by an accident it comes
To the soldier returning home?
Can I rally just one more time
And close this chapter of my life?
Just a chapter – not the end,
Not now, with the book just opened
Once again.

PLEA

God, hear my cry
And help me through this disfigurement!
As Samson lost his strength,
Bald, I'm losing mine.

Who am I now?
Where do I belong?
My life is shattered.
From fragments, can I make it whole?

Choices, forces all around
Pull at me and tear me down.
I do not know which way to turn.
I'll never be the same again.

When the new me does emerge,
Who will she be?
Answer me, answer me,
So I may know
What must wither, what must grow,
So I can find direction now
And a newfound strength,
A better me, a greater self,
A happy soul with no more strife,
With peace of mind
And renewed life!

INVINCIBLE

I am invincible!

My heart, my soul tell me so.

No matter what is done to me

I am in control.

I am the master

Of my physical whole.

There is a guiding energy,

A magic light, a flame within.

No one can quell it,

For it is mine!

I have no more fear.

That fire that burns in me

Gives me strength and gives me life;

With its help

I shall win this fight.

I know that I will heal.

I shall beat disease

Once and for all!

PATIENT'S PLEA
OR
TO MY PHYSICIAN

Dearest physician,
I trust myself to thee.
Please be careful
How you handle me.
Handle me with care and love;
Give me time to comprehend
What you with training understand.
Do not shield me from the truth,
Rather try to feel, yourself,
The weight its meaning brings to bear
Upon my mind and heart.
If your words will sting my soul,
Bestow them gently
And choose them thoughtfully.

Do not steal my dignity.
Though you steer the ship for me,
Let me put my hand, too, upon the wheel
So that I may feel,
I have control.
Though I'm afraid
And so are you,
Do not control me with that fear.
Let us face together the unknown,
In partnership and hope.

The Monster and the Light

What a horrid thing I saw,
When I met head-on with my disease.
That monster evoked a primal scream,
Then anguished sobs came forth.

With sobs and screams, I drove it out,
And then the light rushed inside…
I was completely still, and let it be,
Gentle healing,
A gift received!

ENLIGHTENED CHEMOTHERAPY

Outside my window,
The sunlight on the river
Gleams in the ripples,
Reflecting my own inner light,
Which transforms the chemicals
Coursing through my veins
Into messengers of life.

Inspiration

Last summer,
As I lay dying,
My youngest child beside me slept.
I felt the respirations of his chest
And breathed to their rhythmicity.

As I inspired, the same as he,
I found the reason
I had to be...
For him, my babe, and beloved others,
His father, two sisters, and three brothers.

More than chemotherapy,
He became the breath of life
For me.

WOUNDED WARRIOR

In battle, once I fell
As I felt a spear penetrate my flesh.
But I, the wounded warrior
Brought to the brink of death,
Did not die...
Why?

Who says I must walk wounded,
Martyred on life's battlefield?
If I pull out the piercing shaft
I stand once more erect,
In the glory of myself,
Empowered, beautiful and healed.

Cancer is but a wound,
It is not death itself.
When I can treat it as a friend
And learn its lesson,
It is then, I shall be healed,
As I extract the fateful spear,
And bear my wound,
No more!

I Am With The Angels

I am with the angels,
Flying fearlessly and free;
The love that fills my heart,
Propels me in my flight.
I have danced with death,
And I was not afraid.
The 'whys' of my disease
And the outcome matter not.
I am with the angels
And I shall be all right!

The surgeon makes the cut,
He and I are a team;
My spirit lights upon his hand
And guides it to my cure,
Then I fill my body with white light,
Where diseased organs were.
In the template for tomorrow
I am at peace.
I am with the angels,
And through love, will heal disease!

THE OCEAN BY NIGHT

I breathed to the rhythmic pounding
Of the ocean on the shore –
My heart raced and energy soared.
Two rocks appeared
Symbolic of decision made:
One cloaked in gray,
One bathed in light.

The first was fear and fight that fell away
And sank into the ocean.
The shining light was strength to heal
And rose toward heaven.
Here in the magic of the night,
The moon that shone, the stars above,
Surrounded by all God's love,
I knew I could go on.

Contemplating The Unknown

Do you know what it's like
To know that death will come
And to not know when...
Every day?

We are all going to die,
But why me
Sooner than the rest?
Or will it be thus?

Is the curse of cancer
Just a label,
Just a warning,
Setting me apart from all the others
So I know my own mortality,
Like a wall before me...
Every day?

In a moment
I confront it
And then I look away
To life,
To all I have...
All of us ever has,
Just this moment,
Now!

We cannot read ahead
Before the book of life is done.
Though we're aware
Of what is written there,
Which of us knows
When he will come
To the very last page?

RELEARNED LESSON

"Give up the fight!"
Puzzled, I search
For meaning in these words.
Until – a lesson learned before its time
Slowly creeps into my mind.
Suddenly I understand,
For I have done it once before –
Cancer showed me how
(My suffering has new meaning now).

In the struggles of last summer
I had given up the fight!
It was then I learned
To let the petty details go
So only love filled up my heart,
And I savored each moment I had
To live.
I walked the beaches,
Day and night,
To ward off thoughts of death.
There I saw His light.

Sensing the beauty of the ocean,
Sky, and Mother Earth,
I knelt and kissed the sand,
Thanking God
For the chance He'd given me
To glimpse the exquisiteness
Of all this,
And feel the force
Of Universal Love!

HOPE

Deep within the well of my discouragement

There is yet a drop of hope.

Sparkling in the sun,

It captures the light

Of my strength,

And brings fresh life

To my despairing spirit

Which will flourish,

Giving off the sweet essence

Of my self

In this,

Its new beginning!

LIVING IN THE MOMENT

I shall not waste today into yesterday,

Worrying about tomorrow.

As I open my eyes to all that I have now

And live in the moment,

Laughing, loving, and being loved,

I dance in the face of death

And I will not die!

To Life!
An Affirmation

I celebrate my life!
I know how much it means
And how fragile is the balance
In which it hangs.
I must grab hold of each moment,
Living to the fullest,
For tomorrow may not be.

I shall breathe in with joy,
The earth, the sun, the sky;
I will imbibe the love of my family,
Each and every one.
I cannot let life go
When so much is left undone.

The Light within will guide me,
Shining forth from my self and soul.
I shall make it 'til tomorrow
By living here and now!

To Live Is Not To Die

I will begin each day by living

Now is not the time for dying.

I will love each moment that I live

And savor it for all it is.

Smell the flowers, hear the birds,

Dance with joy,

And even cry,

But never stop to wonder why

There may not be tomorrow.

No place to heal

I sat at my desk and I knew it was wrong
To stay in a system where I no longer belong.
True healing cannot be done by the clock –
This is not how I measure "standard of care!"
To assess how they are feeling
A bond must be formed;
From caring comes trust
And that all takes time.
These third party payers cannot understand –
It is business, not healing, they have in mind.

If I stay in this system, I cannot survive,
For I want really to heal,
To feel for them all,
To reach into their souls
And bring out their smiles,
To help them get well
As they help themselves.

This I shall do,
It is God's work and mine.
If I cannot do it here,
Then I will have to leave...
I shall go where there's time
To do what I must,
To share with the patient
In that moment of trust.
I can guide them to heal,
As I've healed myself,
For I now comprehend
What true medicine is.

DREAMS AND REALITY

WHERE ARE YOU, PETER PAN?

I sobbed so hard my body shook –
Where were Peter and Captain Hook?
Oh, how I cried to realize
That the truth had shut my eyes.
The Never Land was gone,
So, too, were the pirates and the boys.

Oh, Peter Pan,
Where are you now?
Where has imagination flown,
Now that I'm a woman, grown?
Can I no longer fly with you,
As I did once, when I was young?
Are all the wondrous fairies gone –
Can't I believe and clap my hands?
Where are you, Peter Pan?

What a gift little children have –
In their innocence, they can believe
In the wildest runnings of their minds,
And anything can happen!

As an adult, must I lose all this,
The fantasy and the bliss?
No, no, I won't let it be so!
I'll let my inhibition go –
Once more I'll fly with all of them,
With the children...
And with Peter Pan!

MIXED BLESSING

Yesterday, a joy unfettered
Burst forth from me
And leapt into being.
Today there is pause.
Give it back to me!

Joy tempered with sensibility
Is tarnished.
Must it be?
Oh, to feel again that freedom,
Like flying.

But first the rest
Must be dealt with.
There will be tears,
Many tears…

Will full joy follow?
After these shadows fall,
Will there be light?
I have shed my chrysalis,
But must I mourn
Before the butterfly is born?

REALITY AND DREAMS

Yesterday I bumped into reality.

In its realm, my fantasy was gone.

Tears welled up inside,

And I cried.

We need our dreams

To bear the burden of what is real.

Today I wander, lost and sad,

But I know

Tomorrow a new dream will come,

And I shall smile again!

FLIGHT AND FANTASY

In the presence of an angel,

I kiss my dream.

Flying high upon a fantasy,

I must hang on, oh so tight,

So as not to be deterred

By those who would drag me back

To reality!

How To Go On Flying

Where am I now,
In the Never Land?
Are you my Peter Pan?
I feel connected to a world
Beyond the one that others see.
Is this real? Is it me?
Or is this how I escape
Reality?

No, no, go back one step,
My dear,
To all that you've discovered
In one very telling year.
Relax, and breathe, and trust
What you really feel,
Who you really are,
A free and boundless spirit
Connected to the light,
The energy of the earth,
And the universe.

You stand here at the edge
Of a new life.
Seize it now!
Hold on tight,
Believe...
And you will fly with Peter Pan.
The wonderment and joy you feel
Is indeed real.
It is not denial of the truth,
But acceptance of all this:
Your connection to the light,
The energy of earth,
And the universe.

REDISCOVERED SPIRIT

As I have done before,

I take control

And turn my world around.

Yesterday's despair is gone.

The sun has come out again,

And there is beauty everywhere.

Joy makes my spirit soar.

My heart again can sing,

Free and glad,

With zest for life,

And energy recaptured,

As I realize dreams once more!

THE DAWNING OF MY DREAMS

I ride into tomorrow
On the dreams of today.

As the expressions of my inner self
Become reality,
I expand beyond my own belief
Towards new horizons.

Taking a deep breath,
I become exuberant
As I inhale the essence of self-fulfillment
That this moment brings.

ETERNAL PROMISE

As I began to grow
I felt a sadness,
A gnawing fear I'd never feel
The total flowering of my soul.
Sorrow brought the healing tears,
And I lay still and breathed the pain.

A guiding shaft of light
Came straight from God.
It pierced my abdomen
And brought
All His love and energy.

Floating in that luminous burst,
United with the ocean and the earth,
I knew…
I would be all I could
And see my dreams fulfilled,
In this life —
Or the next.
It mattered not.

HEALING THE WOMAN AND THE CHILD WITHIN

BEYOND THE MIND

It is very dark here,
Where I wander
Deep within the caverns
Of my subconscious.
The light that led me here
Has faded now,
As I venture into the farthest reaches
Of my soul.

Both parents come and go,
Escaping in an evanescent memory,
But I perceive only distance,
And exchange no love with them.
Though I long for love,
Love is lacking here,
And my longing goes unanswered.

I touch tears and cannot cry,
Yet I can feel the sadness.
As I explore sensations from the past,
Only fragments can I find.
The rest must wait...
For I have far from finished
My journey beyond the mind.

THE PLACE BEYOND

I walked on the moon,
I stepped into the sun.
I saw a special place beyond,
Lit in blue and gray,
With rocks and birds and figures, vague.

Then came a perfect stillness –
Total silence –
Nothing changed,
As, transfixed
Within the sun,
Held in its bright light,
I could go no further.

It was not for today
To explore the mystery of that space,
Rather just to stay so still
And wait.

THROUGH THE SILENCE I WILL HEAL

I. Sickness And The Sadness

I cry and cry,
And from inside
I suddenly feel the sickness rise.
More than once I choke and gag
Until it is removed at last.
Soon the tears well up again
Leading me deeper within
To a lonesome little girl,
Heartbroken
Because her daddy's gone.

II. Anger And The Question

I sense the anger swell,
I have to yell
As it is held
Within my fisted hand.
Of all that has befallen me,
I question "Why?"
Then in the mystery
God replies.

III. The Answer

In the stillness and the peace
He answers me,
"I love you...
Be not afraid!
Your healing will come
From all this pain.
It is hence you will learn
To heal the ills of man,
With Divine hand
And all the love you hold within.
But you must walk this path alone –
Do not talk away the lessons,
For thus you will dissipate the message."

IV. My Response

As I lie cradled in His sweet embrace,
His love, for my own, becomes the spark,
And I feel it grow within my heart.
Able now to face the dark,
Alone with God
I seek the silence!

A JOURNEY TO SELF

In a sacred moment
I know my truest self,
But then the vision clouds.

I become engulfed
In delusions from the past
Embodied in the persons
Of the men I love the best.

Lost and dizzied,
I struggle back towards center.
Until, guided on the strains of Spirit song,
I return to core star self,
And in its astounding truth
I behold, once more,
The phenomenon of me.

THE HEALING

Having dared to touch the depth of fear,
Suddenly,
My spirit soared.
Split from the center of my heart,
A healing light of Divine love
Emerged.

I felt myself embraced by angels,
Borne ever upward
In their gentlest love,
To a celestial plane
Where, truly healed,
I rested –
Breaching life and death,
Totally at peace
With soul and self.

THE RAPISTS

We have all been raped!
To violate our inner truth
Is obscene –
And all of us are guilty.
When we stare another in the face
And are not true to self,
It is we who are the rapists.

Victims of our own deception,
We betray ourselves;
Our souls cry out
And scream for help.
It is up to us
To hear them,
For there is no salvation
Save from deep within.

HEALING TEARS

Tears keep dropping from your eyes –
You think there is no end in sight.
But as tears fall,
You feel refreshed
And start from yet another place.

For tears are messengers that heal,
Restoring wholeness to your soul.
So let the teardrops fall
Upon your face,
Cleansing toxins from within,
Washing away the awful pain,
Until, just when you think
It is almost gone,
Not fully healed,
You cry again.

LOST

When I should be alive and filled with joy,
All I seem to do is cry.
I have no place to go, no place to hide.

Disease gave me a chance to fly free,
Validating the woman I want to be.
But in physical recovery
I have lost my creative energy.
Am I not entitled
To experience me?

Will the old self now kill the new?
Will I cease to be the new self I have become,
Who right now has no home?

What will I keep and what will I discard?
Where will I go
To live out my dreams?

TEARS OF LONGING, TEARS OF SADNESS

Endless tears betray my longing

To expand infinitely

In expression of myself,

Without any boundary

For my being –

Totally free

To be... to feel... to love,

To have the love returned

In a never-ending circle

Of acceptance,

Where it is safe to need,

And to receive –

As well as give.

Shed, not just in longing

To be all I can,

These tears fall, as well, in sadness

For so much time I should have been

A glorious human being,

Full of beauty and of light,

Not kept crouched in darkness,

Afraid to simply be...

And feel myself accepted

As the essence

Of who I am.

Confrontation With Anger

A black flame
Edged in orange
Darts through me
And bares the anger at my core.

I rage a primal scream of hate...
And of hurt
At those whom I should love.

I fall into a blackened void,
A well of stillness
In the dark side of my soul.

Rage And Tears

Within my soul a darkness stirs,
Slowly growing as I breathe.
It swells into full-blown being –
Rage!

Exploding,
It consumes me in its fire,
Wrought from the very pits of hell.
I strike and thrash,
I bite and scream.
There seems to be no end
To fury.

Over and over
I sense it rise within me,
So long contained,
It will not be tamed.
I must now feel
Its full expression.

Frenzied,
I kick, I flail,
But to what avail?
It changes nothing!
There is only pain,
And in the wake of anger,
Boundless tears
Overflowing
In a tide that knows no ebb,
Until the furor
Rises once again!

INVALID

Invalid,
Crouched, cursed, behind your defensive wall,
Ashamed to need
And to receive,
Forced to believe you must only give,
Who taught you
That you do not deserve the love you crave,
That all your wants
Are...Invalid?

Can I now make the wall come down?
Can I release you from this jail?
How, but by loving you
With all my heart,
Validating who you really are?
Beautiful woman,
Full of love,
Who can receive
And does deserve,
Every bit as much as you so willingly give.

Undaunted,
We are both healing now,
Erasing all the aches and scars,
As together we merge and blessed grow
In the magnificent light
Of all God's love
That guides us to that special place,
Transcending time and death,
Where all is love
And there is no fear,
And we are free to be
Who we truly are.

THE NEW PATHWAY

Choice weighs heavy on my mind:
The road divides
I do not know which way to go.
If I take the old familiar way
I shall betray…myself
And all I have become,
And in so doing might be ill again –
(The newborn baby dies!)

But what about the other path –
Will I get lost and stumble?
There is no shelter but my inner strength.
I see a tiny ray of light.
Is that sufficient guide amidst the shadows
To bring me through the woods?
If I make it through,
I know I'll see the sun
Atop the mountains
Of my dreams!

HEARTBREAK

Love unites me with God.

As I draw in the light,

I hear Him declare His love for me.

But angered at my fate,

I question Him and recoil in hate.

Yet, with a clear-cut answer

To disregard what's transpired,

He calls me His special child...

Until evil creeps under my skin,

And I am engulfed in doubt,

Once again

Questioning, crying out,

"Will His love be enough to heal,

The wounds in my heart

And the pain I feel?"

HELL'S FIRE OR DIVINE FLAME?

A fearsome fire burns,
Enticing me to come within
And yet not be consumed.
Reflecting my hesitation,
The flames freeze
Into a crystalline cavern,
Calling me once again.

I enter and explore
The dimensions of my fear.
Inside terror's cave,
Images parade,
Some dark,
Some ashen gray as death,
Distortions of the truth
That haunt me from the past.

Then, transcending fear,
My heart becomes aflame
With unconditional love.
Sparked by God,
This, my own celestial light,
Will guide me through
Those fear-filled caverns in the night,
As I unite
With all that is
The universe!

Shadows In The Light

I came to you in light
And leave in shadows.
Must it be thus?
Of course!
I knew better when I came...
There are still some tasks undone.

Wounds yet unhealed,
Scars covered up,
Relationships left unresolved,
Are rope enough to bind my soul
To delusions from the past
That choke off my voice
So I'm not fully free to speak
Of love and all the needs I have,
Asking for dreams that I deserve.
I'm too scared to express who I am,
Lest I be wounded
Once again!

If I face this fear head-on,
Loose these ropes that bind me down,
I'll see a light that's brighter still,
Until...
There is another task,
Another spectre from the past.
There are always shadows in the light,
Day cannot dawn
Without the night!

FRAGMENTS OF THE TRUTH

Clarity is dawning.

The fragmented pieces of my existence

Come together as a whole.

As I emerge from the darkness of my fear.

The truth has set me free.

Still trembling with the energy of discovery,

Uplifted by the joy of understanding,

I feel as if I'm floating.

Though there is much more to know,

I've made a small beginning.

The windows of my soul are clearing now

So I may peek therein

At the mysteries the little girl

Has locked away

Into unconscious memory.

RESTLESS CHILD

Looking deep within,

I asked the frenetic child

Why she was always running, running, running, wild.

"Oh little girl, what hurts you so,

That you are always on the go?

It seems your soul just cannot rest –

What is this thing you cannot face?"

"Change," she said, "is scaring me,"

And with her answer began to cry.

I responded, crying, too,

For I felt her pain...

(Which was my own.)

Mourning with her the fading past,

I wept until I fell asleep,

And sleeping let the child be

To grow and heal

With me.

Between Two Worlds

I live in two worlds.
Lost between them,
A woman and a child play.
Who are they?

Some days I am whole and strong,
But then I come apart again.
The old world cries, and says, "Please stay,"
Then the new place beckons me away.

If these worlds could fuse
With elements from each,
I would feel an inner peace,
And deep within my soul,
I'd know I were
Truly whole.

THE TANTRUM AND THE CHILD

There's a child in me
Who won't be still
Or go away,
Who, long ago,
Didn't have her say.
So she carried deep within
The sadness and the pain.
Instead of shedding tears,
A tantrum took control
To keep her feelings cold.

When the woman starts to feel,
It happens once again:
The little girl steps in,
Caught up in a storm.
Feelings stuffed away
Never come into play;
Just as in the past,
They remain unexpressed.

What happened in the past
Must not happen now.
Woman and child are one –
Both have much to learn.
The girl is free to cry,
For the woman understands,
But when the woman feels,
The girl must stay at bay.
Having temper tantrums
Is child's play.

RECONCILIATION

I came upon the little girl,
Crying all alone.
Object of my rejection,
Longing for affection,
She drew forth love from me
I now could not withhold.
Empassioned, we embraced.
I could feel the force of love,
As we two reconciled,
The woman and the child.

I love my new-found self
And this child as well.
She returns the love to me
In a very special way.
Because we love each other,
I do not need another –
I can stand alone,
When the woman and child are one.

She did her work so well,
As I lived life in the past.
There are still jobs for her,
If she'll do them on my terms.
We'll work and live together,
And build from strength, combined.
We'll always share each other,
This little girl and I.

CHANGE AT THE HELM

I watch the little girl
And love her as she plays.
Soon she is replaced –
A green-stone, frozen woman,
Heartbroken and abandoned,
Takes the center stage alone.
I cry for her,
And slip into a deeper state.

As I heal,
In my hand I feel the wheel.
The little girl returns.
She steers the ship,
But not for long.
Once cowering, the woman now stands strong,
Striving for control,
Wrenching the wheel from her –
Now the child lies on the ground,
While the woman takes command.

The light of God brings love
And as the ship sails on
With the woman at the helm,
The girl stands by her side
Enamored, 'neath her arm.

PEACE AND ACCEPTANCE

I cried the pain
Of unrequited love,
But I was wrong,
For in a moment,
All was changed,
And I sensed sweet acceptance come
To the woman that I am,
A beautiful being engulfed in light...
I could feel the living breath
Unite me with the ones just like
Myself.

I brought the little girl with me,
So she, too, perceived the peace.
She no longer had to take control
To force approval
And keep her hold
On those she wanted so
To love her.

She and I could simply be
In union with kindred souls,
Experiencing the force that flowed
Back and forth
From them to us
In a beautiful, peaceful
State of bliss.

LIGHT OUT OF PAIN

"You will find me,"
Is what you said,
Beautiful woman
Rising from my pain…
Somehow I knew
I would.

The light you left behind with me
Will become my soul's energy,
Filling me pregnant with its glow,
Until I know
The endpoint of my dreams.

So I lift my arms,
Embrace the light,
Then, hugging the abstract
I release the love inside of me
And cry –
Because it is, as yet
Unanswered.

RESTORATION

Weakened, deeply saddened,

I begin to search within.

There, shrouded in misconception,

The ghost of my former self

Gasps, clinging to the past.

In one dark moment

A shriek dispels the old beliefs,

And the phantom lady is gone.

In her place another woman

Stands vibrant and reborn.

Clothed in the golden light of God,

She is my new and truer self,

Beautiful and strong!

As I absorb this image,

I am empowered and restored.

Birth And Rebirth

I come to a beautiful field
And there I give birth!
This, my seventh child,
Is myself.
I nurse the babe and hold it close.
The sun shines all around,
And I am glad.

Then...
I stand, a lovely woman
Clothed in white,
And beautiful,
Loved and loving,
Strong and free.
What joy, this wondrous day
Has come to me!

I WALK IN LIGHT

Once more, I walk in light,
No longer captive to perfection's sword
That once cut through my soul
And forced me ever onward.
Unrelenting in its drive,
It tried
To rip out my sweeter self,
To make of me a man
In my own father's image.

Now that shining silver blade
Is swallowed up
Into a brighter light.
Bursting resplendent
from God's love
For all that is, and was,
And ever will be,
It emanates
From deep within my heart and soul,
Sending its radiant glow
Back into the universe
Of which I am a part.

THE WOMAN AND THE FORCE

As I open up and let it in,
From Mother Earth emerges
A force so strong it splits my brain
And sets my soul on fire.
Then I stand
United with all womanhood.

The energy that I receive
Will stay with me now,
Come forth and shine
In a light that is my own,
But derived from force divine.
I feel it as a comfort, too,
To get me through
Life's vicissitudes
Undaunted.

AWAKENING TO WOMANHOOD

Floating in the flowers of femininity,

I roll over and over in sensuous glee,

As the silk, soft petals

Caress my flesh

And kiss me with their sweetness.

My left side sleeps no more,

Awakened in the dawn

Of new fulfillment.

The right side,

Dormant now,

Lies quiet, stark and still –

Its day is done.

In its darkest night

It slumbers.

I was split asunder

So these two sides might part,

And I could choose

To steep my soul

In delicate fancies,

And be reborn...

A woman!

REBORN WOMAN

Free at last
To fly upon my dreams,
I've found her,
The me for whom I'd searched.
I shall dance once more
With joy.
Emancipated and deserving,
My self has found her energy
Again...
To go where she wants to go,
And be all that she will,
Unchained.

How beautiful she is,
This woman laced with light,
Derived from source divine.
But like a babe just born,
I have so much to learn
As I grasp my life anew,
Flying unrestrained.

A PLAYER ON THE STAGE

When I was very young
The curtain fell on creativity.
It is it rising once again.

It's time upon the stage of life
To open up my heart and soul.
I do not need approval or applause –
This, my best performance,
Is for me.

FAMILY

ETERNAL LOVE

I've learned about love that has no end,

Between mother and child, espoused lovers and friends.

Open yourselves to your hearts,

And you, too, will feel it

As we sing and dance and embrace each other.

So hold me in your arms my dearest ones,

And when I must go

Where life is no more,

Weep not,

For we shall share this love

That now binds us in life,

As it transcends even death,

Forever!

LOVE FOREVER

Unconditional love

Between mother and child,

Husband and wife,

And very special friends,

Endures forever,

Indestructible.

It matters not

How far apart

The principals move,

In space...

In time...

And in the continuum

Between life

And Eternity.

BEYOND THE WALLS

Beyond the penetrated walls

Of pseudomotherhood

That you erected,

I behold you,

Dearest mother,

Loving, soft, and tender,

More beautiful than any angel…

As I approach in adoration,

Our hearts and spirits fuse,

And I am reborn,

To know once more

The wonder and the bliss,

Of unconditional love.

Truth, Love, And Tears

I sit within the shadow of the truth,

Embracing my children, one by one,

Encompassed in the sunlight of our love.

Joy bursts from my heart,

But tears spill forth as well,

As I share with each of them,

A piece of myself.

WHO IS NORMAL?

What is hidden

In the closets of our minds?

What would you see

In intimacy

With the finest family?

Do the pillars of the community

Come tumbling down

Behind closed doors?

What pain and tears

Are lurking behind the smiles

On the faces

Of those we hold in high esteem?

Who's dysfunctional

And who is not?

What wounds inflicted on our children now

Will open in the years to come...

And who inflicted them on us?

So then, what is normality?

Who's to say –

You...

Or me?

THE CLEARING STORM

Foreboding clouds are closing in.

My trepidation grows

As dark and evil

Envelop me.

I must escape,

Yet I do not leave,

For something holds me here.

I breath in the light

To clear the storm...

The clouds lift,

Leaving a cleansed emptiness

And then an inner peace.

Storm clouds gather once again.

Stalwart, I stay,

And as I breathe,

The light reappears

As a concentrated band of energy,

Molten metal flowing from my heart

To those who have most meaning.

I ask of them forgiveness.

As we commingle in the light,

There is between us

Only love.

MOTHER'S LAMENT

Once there were six,
Now only three,
Soon there will be none,
And I'll be alone.
When they were young,
I didn't savor enough
Of the precious moments we had
And now they are gone.

How quickly they flew,
The years of their youth.
Time stole them from me –
It was over so soon.
I can't bring them back
Except in my dreams,
In the memories I have
As I look into their eyes.

I look into their eyes,
And mine fill with tears,
As they have matured,
I have grown old.
Oh, where have they gone,
The years of my youth?

GROWTH

My soul awakens,

Naked.

I have shed my skin once more.

Unprotected, must I now go,

Without you,

Reaching new horizons

On my own?

There are familiar tears

Of mourning for the old,

Which once was new,

Replacing what was then

So I could grow,

As now I shall again.

DON'T CRY, MY LOVE

In the freeing of myself
I have begun by hurting you.
Don't cry, my love,
It is inevitable.
Don't you know
She had to go,
The old, dependent being,
Clinging to your identity,
Unable to assume her own,
She walked a different path.

Now, from strength I come,
Strength that is my own.
I am a beautiful woman
Shining in the light
Of my inner self.

A MOTHER'S LOVE

In a vision that I had,
I took each child of mine by the hand,
And, one by one, I let them go
To feel the freedom in their souls.

Then I beheld them,
Never gone,
Arms outstretched to touch my own,
Giving back to me
The very love
That set them free.

FURY TAMED

Sad and angry, full of fear,
I rage upon the ones I love,
Struggling for the strength to live,
Despite the odds I know I have.

I try in vain to quiet the rage,
But I must play it out until it's done.

Now the fury's gone.
As I lie here in your arms
In the stillness of our love,
I am at peace.

Invitation On Our 28th Anniversary

Come now, my dearest, and feel with me

The essence of our love,

That which from a tiny spark

Has become an eternal flame.

Let its warmth pervade your being,

As it does my own,

And you will see how we are held

In a Divine circle of light,

Our souls and spirits fused

In everlasting wedlock

That will never be undone!

Pyramid Of Light

Oh pyramid of light,
In this, my darkest night,
Send down your energy,
Remove me from this cloud
Of anger and of fright.
Now rain the endless tears
Of compassion and of love
For those I hold so dear.
Though this be not my fight,
I am here to comfort and to guide,
To lend support, and point the way
To the road that I once walked,
From darkness
Into light!

ENLIGHTENMENT

MIRACLE ON THE BEACH

As I walked the beach,
The late afternoon sun
Cast my shadow on the sand.
Alone with the sea,
I opened up my heart and cried,
Releasing the anguish
Of what might be lifetimes.
I walked off the pain for miles on end,
As I tried to approach an elusive dune
Which seemed to evade me as I came near.
Finally I attained its forbidden top.
There I stood and talked to God.

As I watched the evening sun descend,
Surrounded by ocean, sun and sand,
I sensed His wonders everywhere.
Suddenly all the pain was gone.
I was part of this miraculous whole,
And inside myself I felt truly healed.
I could grasp life, and face even death.
I knew God was with me,
And I would always be safe!

A SPECIAL UNION

I inhale the water and the air.

My spiritual lungs inflate

With joy.

The beauty that I see around me

Fuses with my soul,

As I become

One

With nature and the universe,

Part of that great design

Created by a Higher Power

Whose energy I feel within myself,

A Divine light

Radiating outward

And making me unique,

As I walk my path

Within the world

That others know.

On The Wings Of The Owl

On the wings of the owl,
I flew with the wind
Close to the sun.
As her heart beat,
So also did mine
At the breathtaking beauty
Confronting our eyes:
Leaves brushed my cheeks
In the forest below –
Windblown sands in the desert
Shed a purplish glow,
Sun-laced clouds parted
And an angel appeared,
Then finally shone
The bright light of God.

God's Answers

Cushioned in Divine love,

As angels hold my hands,

I enter a new Kingdom,

An even higher place

Than I have known before,

A place of total peace.

Here I let go,

And in a state of fullest trust,

I feel myself at one with the Great Spirit,

Accepting that I cannot have all answers now,

But knowing when, in time,

The answers come,

They will be right!

The Ultimate Lesson

Caught between East and West,

I long for life,

But I am trapped in the intimations of death.

Seeds of doubt,

Sown deep in the soil of my training,

Have become the roots of fear.

Entwined therein,

I struggle to be free,

To grow along that greater pathway

That leads into the Light,

Whence comes

God's guiding answer

Of no answer...

"There are no givens,

Not even death.

You must simply trust –

For this, your greatest lesson

In unconditional love

Is between yourself

And Me!"

WITH MY BODY AND MY HEART

*".....And thou shalt love the Lord, thy God, with all thy
heart, with all thy soul, with all thy might."*

(Deut. IV, 4-9.)

God took me as a lover,

And with all my body,

I did love Him.

In sensuous awakening

From my loins to my lips,

Spirit rose within me

And taught me how to love,

As my body spoke the language

Of my heart.

Universal Light

Mother Earth's sweet healing energy
And God's empowering light
Become the unconditional love
That draws together everything within the universe
And makes each one of us
A hologram
Of all that is.

Dr. Lesley (Bunim) Heafitz was born October 28, 1940 in New York City. The wife of Dr. Morton Heafitz, she is the mother of Betsy Catya, Joseph Philo, Avrum Scott, Sally Robin, David Ron and Jonathan Michael. The family lives in Swampscott, Massachusetts and summers on Plum Island, off Newburyport. A practicing pediatrician, she is a graduate of Barnard College and Harvard Medical School. Dr. Heafitz is an award-winning, published poet and an amateur thespian. She shared her experiences in dealing with cancer in "The Empathic Way," an address at Harvard Medical School Alumni Day. An instructor at her alma mater, Dr. Heafitz is an inspiration to many.